# EVERYDAY LIFE IN
# IMPERIAL ROME

**PATENTED SYSTEM**

**To watch the full video**
**"A virtual tour from Colosseum to St. Peter"**
▶ use your computer or Smart TV to go to the following
website: www.archeolibri.it/it/video/vita-quotidiana.html
The password is: **dqsdi7a9**
▶ use your tablet or smartphone
to photograph the QR code ➤

# INTRODUCTION: THE BOOK'S STRUCTURE

*This book intends to guide the reader along an imaginary journey into ancient Rome, in one of the most splendid periods of its history.*

*The tour will bring the reader to explore the city in the year 80 AD, ideally on the day of the inauguration of the Flavian amphitheatre, better known as the Colosseum.*

*Along the way, windows will open onto both historical themes and descriptions of everyday life, to provide a complete picture of life in the capital of the Roman Empire and its extraordinary "modernity". The main characteristics of the book are its beautiful **illustrations of reconstructions** which overlap onto the pictures of today's Rome to offer the reader an authentic plunge into the past, showing what it would have looked like in antiquity.*

> **Narration:** the story follows the spectators on the first day of the games at the Colosseum, in an itinerary across the city exploring the history, customs and traditions of Rome.

**Focus box:** this is indicated by square icons, which illustrate the contents. These may refer to themes regarding periods subsequent to the 1st Century AD, relating however to the subject dealt with.

---

> *The surprising interiors of the Colosseum*

*Everyone, when entering, could see the vast arena that extended in the central part of the building, which on that day of the inauguration was not yet completed. It looked like a sort of basin which could have easily been filled with the water from the underground aquifer. For this first event though the basin would be covered by wooden boarding on which the inaugural spectacle would take place.*

*In years to come, spectators could admire ship battles (naumachiae), like the ones that were held in other Roman venues.*

*It was only a few years after the inauguration of the Colosseum that Domitian built the complex underground network (see box on p. 51), which enabled a perfect organization of the entertainment.*

## ONE HUNDRED DAYS OF SPECTACLES

The hundred days for the celebrations of the inauguration of the Colosseum have been described to us by Roman authors of subsequent periods. About twenty years later Svetonius, in his "Life of Titus" writes that no less than five thousand wild animals were fought in just one day. About a century later instead, the historian Dion Cassius writes about a spectacular battle between cranes and four elephants and that about nine thousand animals and two thousand gladiators were killed. These weren't the only extraordinary numbers: under Trajan, in the venationes (hunts) held in the **Colosseum**, in 120 days, 11,000 animals from every part of the vast empire had fought for their lives.

50
I.

*Reconstruction of the Colosseum. Hunting scene (venatio) in the arena.*

The reconstructions are the result of a careful analysis of historic documents, integrated with the interpretation of the publishers and the imagination of the artists.

On the whole, a popular criterion was adopted but always respectful of the fundamental historic elements of academic research and at the same time responding to the needs of the reader.

## THE COLOSSEUM BASEMENTS

The amphitheatre's dense underground network of chambers and tunnels was used to host the games' protagonists, gladiators, beasts, and all that was necessary for the combats and hunts. This underground level extended throughout the whole area, divided into four quadrants by two large corridors that crossed in the centre. This enabled a perfect organization, thanks to which the games took place in the arena with maximum efficiency. There were even large hoists for lifting the beasts and the necessary equipment up to the arena level, while the gladiators used a passage that connected this underground area to the adjacent smaller amphitheatre, the *Ludus Magnus*, built for them to train in.

Another underground level presented a ring shaped water piping connected to the aquifer which had generated Nero's lake; it was used, as well as for washing out the arena, also for the amazing water shows created before the construction of the underground level and described with admiration by the authors of the time, such as Svetonius, Martial, Dion Cassius.

*Reconstruction of the hoist mechanism in the Colosseum underground level.*

**Peculiarity Box:** peculiarities regarding the focus themes framed in boxes with the icon of the theme of reference incorporated in a round logo.

Thanks to the **QR codes** on the rear of the illustrations, it is possible to view 11 short videos on smart-phone or tablet showing interesting analyses and reconstructions related to the subjects dealt with.

# Crowds heading towards the Colosseum

>>>>>>>>>>>>>>>>>>>>>>>>>>>>>>>>>>>>>>>>>>>>>>>>>>>>>>>>>>>>>>>>>>>>>>>>

*In the glorious June sun, in that distant Roman year 833 (year 80 AD), the city awoke in anticipation of a memorable event: the inauguration of the huge amphitheatre that Emperor Vespasian had started building in 71 AD in the vicinity of the **Roman Forum** and which in that day was being inaugurated by his son Titus, risen to the throne about a year earlier. Though some of the interiors were unfinished and had been left in wood to accelerate the inauguration ceremony, the structure was built entirely in masonry, differently to the previously built amphitheatre of Statilius Taurus in Campus Martius, which was destroyed – because it was built in wood – in Nero's fire sixteen years earlier.*

*The flow of spectators from the different areas of the metropolis towards the huge arena (which could seat over 70,000 people), couldn't have been too smooth considering the narrow streets of Rome (see box pages 8-9)*

*Unlike the many other cities built in the territories of the Empire, with their typical straight roads, a heritage of the military encampments, the capital had preserved the greater part of the republican centre, with narrow undulating roads climbing up the city's hills. The crowds were mixed: young boys, mature men, and even a great many women, donning a vast collection of Roman atire (see box p. 10-11).*

page 12 >>

*View of the Colosseum, the Sacred Way and the Arch of Constantine.*
**The Colosseum, the day of its inauguration (80 AD).** ➤

# THE STREETS OF ROME: TRAFFIC

The streets of Rome were often congested not only by traffic, but because of the great number of shops and stalls, with street traders offering their merchandise to passers-by, often causing traffic jams.

There was plenty of confusion in spite of the law that had been enforced for more than one hundred and twenty years, emanated by Caesar to establish rigorous traffic hours, allowing in the daytime only the circulation of means of transport for people, the litters. These were a sort of mobile bed for wealthy Romans carried by at least four slaves (but even as many as eight).

The means of transport of goods instead could only circulate at night. It is easy to imagine how this must have caused great annoyance due to the noise at night: however, the decree had remained in force and would be for a long time to come.

# PEDESTRIAN CROSSING

For pedestrians to safely cross the roads, which were always congested with traffic and periodically flooded at night to wash away the dirt, Rome's streets had blocks of stone strategically placed as stepping stones.

# ROMAN GARMENTS

Roman clothing was typically very simple. The basic item was the tunic, a rectangular gown, tied at the waste with a belt. On top of that men wore the toga which could be a *toga praetexta* (with crimson trimming worn by the political authorities and adolescents) and the *toga virilis* (completely white) worn by adult men.

Both would be draped around the body leaving the right arm free, and this often required the help of a slave. During the Imperial Age, the ancient use of the toga in everyday life was replaced by the *pallium*, a shorter and more practical garment.

The women's tunic, unlike that of men, was ankle length.

Over the tunic, women wore a stole, a rectangular cloth (the *stola*), but when they walked the streets women would wear the *palla*, an ample cloak with which they would also cover their head.

There was also a great passion for jewellery, supreme sign of elegance of the Roman matrons.

Children's clothing was very similar to that of the adults.

Their only characteristic was the *bulla*, a medallion placed around their neck a few days after their birth, which all children of the free people could wear. It was removed on their seventeenth birthday, in a rite of passage to adulthood and offered to the domestic Lars (the Gods who protect the home) in the ceremony of the change of toga from *praetexta* to *virilis*.

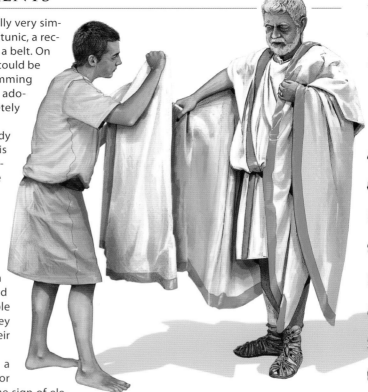

*Glass ampullae for containing perfumes. Dressing in the toga praetexta.*

*Above, portrait of a woman of imperial age on wooden panel.*

## > *Crossing the Roman Forum*
>>>>>>>>>>>>>>>>>>>>>>>>>>>>>>>>>>>>>>>>>>>>>>>>>>>>>>>>>>>>>>>

*People coming from the north and western districts of the city approached the valley where the new amphitheatre stood, crossing the ancient monarchic-republican Forum. This was by now crowded with edifices, temples, statues, honorary columns, but also shops, taverns, street vendors peddling their merchandise to the crowds of passers-by. The old Forum had kept its original appeal, that of a bustling, lively centre.*

*In the **Aemilia and Julia Basilicas**, where justice was administered (see box below) it was a business day as usual. There were plenty of citizens who were interested in following judicial proceedings and were willing to wait hours for the trial to begin, sitting on the steps outside the building, playing on the chessboard engraved in the travertine steps.*

>>

## ADMINISTRATION OF JUSTICE

Before the hearing, the parties would consult a legal expert (a jurist) to discuss the procedures and the nomination of the judge. Then the actual trial took place, which started with the pleadings of the counsels for the prosecution and for the defence, followed by depositions from the witnesses. The following day, the proceedings usually ended with the rulings of the jury; in particularly complex cases however, it was possible to obtain rather lengthy deferments.

The judges of the penal cases were selected with particular care amongst the most expert magistrates; judgement of the more serious cases, for crimes that were normally punished with the death sentence, was passed by the Senate and, in imperial times, by the same Emperor.

*Marble bust of Marcus Tullius Cicero (politician, orator and a man of letters of the 1st Century BC), Capitoline Museums, Rome. View of the Roman Forum. Chessboard engraved on the steps of the Basilica Julia.*

An extremely significant moment in the history of Roman law was the issuing of the *XII Tables* (approximately 450 BC), which we can somehow consider as the most ancient constitutional charter in history. Up until the publication of *Justinian's Corpus*, this was the only basic code for administering justice in Rome, and was subject to different interpretations.

*Above, fresco by Cesare Maccari, 1839 "Cicero denounces Catilina", Palazzo Madama, Rome.*
*Reconstructed view of the Basilica Julia in the Roman Forum.*

## > Bustling activity in the Roman Forum

Though Caesar, Augustus and later Vespasian had built their Imperial forums with costly extravagance, the importance of the **Roman Forum** remained supreme.

The streets that branched out from the ancient piazza were flanked with shops of all kinds, amongst which the currency exchange stores concentrated near the **Temple of the Dioscuri**. Between the latter and the **Basilica Julia** was the crowded street of **Vicus Tuscus**, so called because it dated back to the Tarquinians, the Etruscan sovereigns of Rome. There was an array of the most disparate shops, from the popular fishmongers, to game and fruit vendors to the aristocratic jewellers, art workshops and bookshops which often held literature readings.

Some activities, like that of barbers (tonsores) were held mainly outdoors: it is easy to imagine, therefore, the hubbub of masculine voices, considering also that it was a Roman custom for men to do the shopping even of daily victuals.

\>\>

*Reconstructed view of the Roman Forum. Roman jewels from Pompeii.* **The Vicus Tuscus in the Roman Forum. ➤**

## > A view of the Curia

>>>>>>>>>>>>>>>>>>>>>>>>>>>>>>>>>>>>>

*Also the solid building of the **Curia**, seat of the Roman Senate (see box below) attracted the attention of the passing crowds.*

*The ancient institution which it housed, after enduring hard times under emperors such as Caligula and Nero, and the brief but hectic period of unrest following the death of the latter, had regained its prestige and security following the conciliatory policies between the imperial power and the ancient institutions – amongst which the Senate – promoted by Vespasian.*

>>

S·P·Q·R

## THE ROMAN SENATE

Created according to tradition by the founder of Rome, Romulus, who selected 100 citizens to form the city's first legislative assembly, the senate accompanied all the transformations of the Roman State, from monarchy to republic and ultimately empire. During the republican period the first main senatorial duties were established; to manage public affairs, present law proposals, stipulate alliances, declare war. Apart from its institutional role, the senatorial class was dominant in Roman society. Every five years an official list was made of its members, new senators were elected and those who proved to be unworthy of the prestigious position were expelled. The assemblies would be held only in sacred buildings and usually took place in the *Curia* within the Roman Forum. At the beginning of the imperial age, though Augustus had left the Senate's role formally unchanged, the senate began to lose its power. Vespasian, with the *Lex de imperio Vespasiani* promulgated when he rose to power in 69 AD, established the new relations between the Emperor and the ancient assembly, relations that each sovereign interpreted according to his fancy. During the period of the empire's decline, the increasing importance of the military led to the natural consequence of a further loss of power, which survived for less than a century from the fall of the Roman Empire (476 AD) up to the Greco-Gothic war (535-553 AD).

*The Curia in the Roman Forum. Bust of Emperor Vespasian.*
*Inscription on a plinth near the Capitol: S(enatus) P(opulus) Q(ue) R(omanus).*

# A CONSUL HORSE?

The prestigious senatorial institution went through difficult periods over the centuries, amongst which, as we have seen, those characterized by the hostility of the imperial power. For example, during his short reign (37-41) Caligula lead a ruthless repression of his internal opposition and purposefully humiliated the senatorial class.

Some historians of Antiquity (all but impartial, such as Svetonius), report a curious episode regarding this Emperor of the Julius-Claudius dynasty, depicted as a bloodthirsty madman. It is in fact Svetonius who writes that Caligula gave his horse *Incitatus* a house with servants; he then adds that there had been rumours according to which he intended to make his horse a consul (but this did not happen).

*Interiors of the Curia; Marble bust of Emperor Caligula.*

## > In the "ultramodern" Imperial Forums

>>>>>>>>>>>>>>>>>>>>>>>>>>>>>>>>>>>>>>>>>>>>>>>>>>>>>>>>>>>>>>>>>>>>>

*It wasn't just the ancient monarchic-republican Forum that captured the attention of the crowds in the slow walk towards the Colosseum. In the part of the valley that extended between the Quirinal, the Esquiline and the same Forum, were the new **Imperial Forums**, the monumental piazzas built to glorify the sovereigns of Rome. The first, created over a century before by Julius Caesar, who had dedicated it to Venus, the divine mother of his family, had been finely built and at great expense though it was not too large. It was dominated by the elegant temple dedicated to the Goddess mother of the Julian family, supreme symbol of beauty. From one of the shops which opened onto the side streets of the **Forum of Caesar**, came a buzzing of children's voices: this was one of the many Roman schools (see box on p.21), its classes held amidst the bustle, the shops and porches.*

*People in the crowd commented on the recent education reform promoted by Titus' father, Emperor Vespasian, who had appointed the great Quintilian to implement a revolutionary initiative: the institution of state schools, funded by the aerarium.*

*View of the Imperial Forums. Statue of Venus, Capitol Museums, Rome.*

## WRITING TOOLS

The Romans wrote on papyri (the expensive parchment made of animal skin was used only for valuable texts or documents) using bird feathers or pointed straws. In schools or for taking notes, they would write on a wooden board with a waxed surface which they engraved with a stylus; the writing could be erased and the board reused a number of times.

Books were actually rolls of parchments which were not too practical to consult; only in the imperial age were the "codes" realized, which presented a succession of pages similar to that of modern books.

## ROMAN SCHOOLS

Basic education (reading, writing and arithmetic) which was quite widespread in ancient Rome, was taught by modest teachers, often self taught, who held classes wherever they could: in the back of a shop or even under a porch, whereas the children of the wealthy families had private tutors. As for higher education, in the 2nd century BC schools were opened with two categories of teachers: grammarians, who taught literature to the younger students, and *rhetores* who taught older students the art of rhetoric (the practical expression of which was oratory, a necessary skill for politicians and lawyers). But these were private schools, up until Vespasian's reform implemented by famous *rhetor,* Quintilian, who became the first state school teacher in history.

*Pompeian fresco depicting Paquius Proculus and his wife, 1ˢᵗ Century, Naples, National Archaeological Museum.*
*Bas-relief of a school scene, end of the 2ⁿᵈ Century AD.*

# > *A changing scenery*

>>>>>>>>>>>>>>>>>>>>>>>>>>>>>>>>>>>>>>>>>>>>>>>>>>>>>>>>>>>>>>>>>>>>>>>>

*The narrow passage in front of the* **Forum of Caesar,** *between the slopes of the Capitol Hill and the Quirinal Hill, formed a bottleneck for the spectators coming in from Campus Martius. Only a few years later, Domitian, Titus' brother and successor, would launch important works here, excavating the banks of this saddle, works which will be completed by Trajan to make room for the grand Forum that bears his name.*

*A panoramic backdrop to this forum was the* **Trajan Market** *which hosted shops of all kinds and taverns, the tabernae, where one could eat (see box on pages 26-27).*

page 28 >>

*The Trajan column. Reconstructed model of the view over the Trajan Forum, Rome, Museum of Roman Civilization. Bust of Emperor Trajan.*                    ***The Trajan markets.*** ➤

# EATING OUT AND AT HOME

Romans had three main meals. Breakfast was quite frugal: generally consisting of bread and cheese and vegetables, but also leftovers from the abundant dinner of the previous day.

At lunchtime they would have a snack, often in taverns (called *tabernae, thermopolia, popilia*), which were frequented by both locals and foreigners, with their embedded wine jars and display of the most popular foods, all at reasonable prices.

At home, the most important meal of the day was dinner. The poorer people ate simple dishes, whereas the wealthier classes began their dinner in the afternoon and ended far into the night. In the high ranking *domus*, a feature of great importance was the dining room for evening banquets, the *triclinium*. Fundamental elements of the decor were the three beds arranged in a U-shape, on which three dinner guests would eat lying down, resting on one elbow.

There were no forks, but they used their hands instead; for this reason at the end of the meal the guests would be brought bowls of water to wash their hands. During the banquet the guests were entertained with song and dance, poetry readings and storytelling.

*Charred bread loaf, 79 AD, Pompeii. Scene of a banquet in the triclinium. Tavern in ancient Ostia.*

Ancient Romans ate simple foods, some of which are today unknown. Amongst the foods which we are less familiar with was the *garum*, very popular amongst Romans, a fermented fish pickle, with a very strong smell, used as a condiment to most dishes.

The most popular foods were vegetables, fruit, eggs, cheese, fish, flat bread, olives, lentils, emmer, barley, farm animal meat and small game. In important banquets instead the most elaborate dishes were made with pork, beef, big game, abundant spices, oysters, fried desserts and nuts. Wine was usually diluted with water and flavoured with honey, spices and aromas. Only

rarely would they serve the *merum,* a pure wine, only of the finest brand (like Falerno, Cecubo, Albano, Sabino, etc.) celebrated by authors such as Plinium and Horatio.

## APICIUS' RECIPES

We have various descriptions of Roman cuisine, in particular in the *"De re coquinaria"* written in the Third Century which is a collection of three hundred recipes attributed to the famous Apicius, who lived under Augustus and Tiberius. The collection, divided into five books, describes food preservation, the preparation of sauces and simple dishes (such as soups and meat pies) and unusual and elaborate dishes (such as flamingos and dromedary calluses), creating a combination of flavours which the Romans found mouth-watering but which are at times difficult for a modern palate to appreciate.

*Fresco from Pompeii depicting a bakery, Naples, National Archaeological Museum.*
*Fresco with game and fruit.*

## > From the markets to the temple

>>>>>>>>>>>>>>>>>>>>>>>>>>>>>>>>>>>

Further ahead one could admire the **Temple of Mars Avenger,** that dominated the **Forum of Augustus** on the background of the powerful wall of fire refractory Gabine stone. The building had been erected to protect the sacred temple from the tremendous fires that continued to break out in the slum district behind known as the Subura, which means "under fire".

Emperor Titus had ordered that before opening the Games homage should be paid to the Gods of this majestic temple. Roman religion (see box in p. 32-33) in fact, was strongly bound to civil life.

Another great attraction was the more recent of the imperial piazza's, the Forum of Peace. This was an imperial piazza which Vespasian had built to preserve the precious treasure plundered from Jerusalem, after his victory in the Judaic war, which included, amongst others, the seven branched candelabra and the Arch of the Alliance.

Here the Emperor had displayed, for all Romans to enjoy, the masterpieces of Greek art which Nero had jealously kept safe in his palace – the Domus Aurea – that has been wiped out from the face of Rome.

page 34 >>

Statue of Mars, Capitoline Museums, Rome. Detail of Titus' Arch depicting the spoils of victory over the conquest of Jerusalem. Women bringing offerings. **Ceremony of Emperor Titus at the temple of Mars Avenger in the Forum of Augustus. ➤**

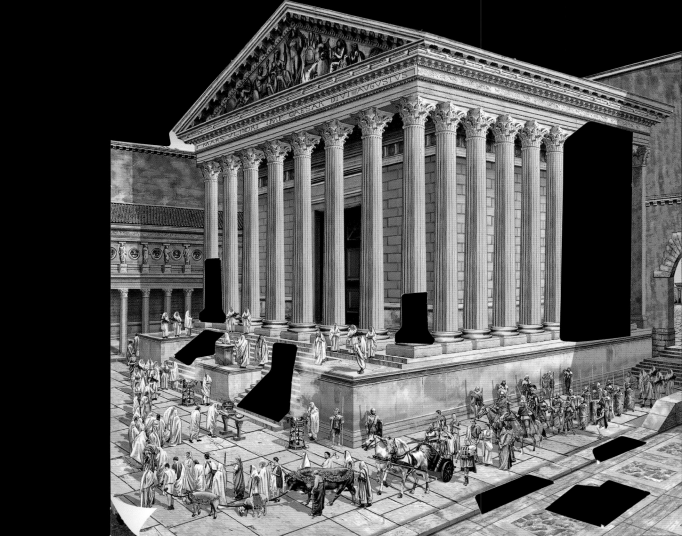

# RELIGION

As in other great civilizations of Antiquity, Rome had a polytheistic religion, with a number of Gods which in the first stage of Roman history personified natural phenomena. Religious practices consisted essentially in rituals, in which domestic animals were sacrificed, for attracting divine favours or placating divine wrath.

These divinities, associated with the world of nature, shared common elements with religions of the populations of Indo-European origin. Years later, as Rome extended its power, the Romans started attributing to the Gods of the populations which were being subjugated, a correspondence with their own divinities. Of decisive impact was then the conquest of Greece and the contemporaneous increase in the influence of Greek culture. The twelve "twin Gods" were thus identified and attributed the same characteristics.

Firstly, the three Gods that formed the "Capitoline Triad", Jupiter (the Greek *Zeus*), Juno (*Hera*), Minerva (*Athena*), and then also Mars (*Ares*), Phoebus (*Apollo*), Venus (*Aphrodites*), Diana (*Arthemides*), Nep-

*Statue representing the Capitoline Triad (Minerva, Jupiter and Juno), Archaeological Museum of Palestrina.*
*Reconstruction of the Temple of Venus Mother in the Forum of Caesar.*

tune (*Poseidon*), Bacchus (*Dionisius*), Mercury (*Hermes*), Vulcano (*Ephestus*), Cerere (*Demetra*). In the Imperial age, religious ceremonies accentuated their political character, due to the divinization of Emperors. At the same time the lessening of ancient beliefs led to the introduction of a series of new oriental cults, such as Mythraism. This disappeared with the growing influence of Christianity until the latter's final victory in the 4th Century under Constantine.

But the all Roman cult of the Lares and Penates remained intact. First come the ancestors, protectors of the family, represented at the entrance of the *domus* by statues placed in a special niche known as the *lararium*. The Penates instead were the spirits, these too protectors, similar to our guardian angels.

# HOUSE OF THE VESTAL VIRGINS AND VESTA'S TEMPLE

The **House of the Vestal Virgins** is located in the Roman Forum behind the Regia – residence of the first kings whose daughters were originally the Vestals. They were virgins devoted to the cult of Vesta, and for this reason, their home was attached to the adjacent temple dedicated to this goddess.

Their task was to never let the sacred flame of the Goddess die and to officiate her cult. They would remain vestals until they were 30 years old and benefitted from a condition of prestige and exceptional political and social rights in Roman society.

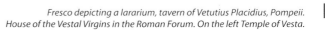

*Fresco depicting a lararium, tavern of Vetutius Placidius, Pompeii.*
*House of the Vestal Virgins in the Roman Forum. On the left Temple of Vesta.*

## > *In the piazza in front of the Colosseum*

>>>>>>>>>>>>>>>>>>>>>>>>>>>>>>

*The crowds had by now filled the vast area obtained from the demolition of the edifices of the **Domus Aurea**, built only fifteen years earlier by Nero around an artificial lake, now replaced by the amphitheatre. Only remaining feature was the grand vestibule that contained the Colossum, the enormous statue that celebrated Nero, which Vespasian had renamed Helios, the God of the Sun. The equally monumental cone shaped fountain had also been restored: this had been built under Augustus and is similar to the "metas" that marked the limits of the Spina of the great circuses. The water, instead of spurting up, trickled gently down from the top (as if sweating), and for this reason was called the **Meta Sudans**.*

*Senators on their litters would weave through the anonymous crowd and other notable citizens – which had the front rows of the amphitheatre reserved to them and their retinue of clientes (see box below).*

>>

## THE CLIENTES: TYPICAL SIGNS OF PRIVILEGE

The *clientes* were citizens who depended entirely on a patron of elevated rank, even though they were not employed by him. This is a social relation unknown to modern society, which in Ancient Rome highlighted the prestige of the upper classes. Normally the *cliente* would present himself early in the morning at the *domus* of his protector, where he would receive food and then also a fixed fee, known as *sportularia*. In exchange, the *cliente* would support his patron in his political campaigns and follow him in his public addresses. The more *clientes* there were, the more important the patron appeared.

*Hypothetical reconstruction of the Meta Sudans. The square in front of the Colosseum, with the Colossus Nero and the Meta Sudans.*

## > Before the amphitheatre: the Domus Aurea

>>>>>>>>>>>>>>>>>>>>>>>>>>>>>>>>>>>>>>>>>>>>>>>>>>>>>>>>>>>

*Since entrance procedures were quite complicated, while they waited people would gaze around at the remarkable changes made to this vast area. Many remembered that only a few years back this area was inaccessible to the population: this was, in fact, part of Nero's incredible palace, the **Domus Aurea**, which after the fire of 64 AD had extended over entire neighbourhoods of the city with pavilions, woods, porticos, imperial gardens. The Flavii had ordered the demolition of the majority of those loathed wonders. But they were still the topic of lively conversation in which insults were hurled at Nero, with definitions such as "matricide" and "arsonist", even though this bad name was not entirely deserved (see box below).*

>>

# DOES NERO DESERVE SUCH A BAD NAME?

Nero has been in the past decades unexpectedly rehabilitated. This stems from a more in depth study of the documents which, without denying his notorious vices, have shed light on positive elements of his actions, especially in economic and social policies. But it was in fact the latter that aroused the aversion of historians of the time, amongst whom, Tacitus, who in the *Annales* writes how the Emperor, intolerant of his mother's interference in affairs of state and accusing her of conspiring against him, ordered her death in a procured shipwreck. The same Tacitus though, expresses strong doubts on the accusation that had Nero setting fire to Rome with devastating consequences in 64 AD, made by another historian, Svetonius and by others. According to the accusers, Nero wanted to burn down whole districts of the city to reclaim huge spaces on which to build his splendid palace, the **Domus Aurea.** The Emperor accused the Christians of having caused this tragic event and subjected them to the first persecution in history. For this reason he was represented by Christian authors as the greatest adversary to the new religion, even though, in actual fact, this primacy can be attributed to some of his successors.

*Marble bust of Emperor Nero. Hypothetical reconstruction of an interior of the Domus Aurea.*
*Painting by Jan Styka, 1900, "Nero in Baia".*

## > In the vicinity of the amphitheatre: the baths

*Emperor Titus had decided to spare the private baths of the Domus Aurea from destruction and open them to the public after appropriate conversion and extension. It's new public status was highlighted by the grand stairs, about 18 metres wide, which allowed one to comfortably reach the baths from the Colosseum level. These were most inviting for the spectators during the intervals in the long days of the games, who would follow the typical bath itinerary (see box 37) which exploited the efficient heating system (see box below).*

*About a century and a half later Titus' Baths were used as a model on which to build the grand **Caracalla Baths** (see box on p.38).*

## THE HEATING SYSTEM

The hypocaust system, used in the beginning of the First Century AD, was based on a pavement suspended on short 60cm brick pillars (*suspensurae*). Hot air produced by a furnace with hatch was channelled into the cavity thus created. The heat in this way was spread to the rooms above, without combustion fumes invading the rooms, which was what happened with the old system of movable braziers. From the second half of the First Century AD, Romans started building cavity walls which enabled heating of larger rooms.

*Reconstruction of a hypocaust heating system.*

# THE BATHS' ITINERARY

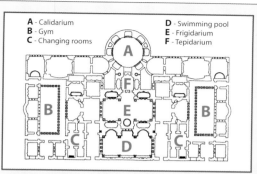

**A** - Calidarium
**B** - Gym
**C** - Changing rooms
**D** - Swimming pool
**E** - Frigidarium
**F** - Tepidarium

The sequence of halls within the thermal baths follows a precise itinerary: the entrance leads to a vestibule onto which one accesses the changing rooms (*apodyteria*). Then there is an outdoor gym, surrounded by rooms for gymnastics and exercise; to one side are a series of complementary rooms. At this point the user, having exercised and enjoyed massage and other accessory services, would step into the round plan *calidarium*, the heated room. From the *calidarium* one passed on to the *tepidarium*, a tepid, slightly smaller room, for an intermediate acclimatization, before stepping into the *frigidarium*, the indoor cool room. In the warm season, instead, the invigorating cold bath took place in the outdoor pool or *natatio*, last leg of the central section.

*Plan of the Caracalla Baths. Women's changing room within a thermal baths complex.*

# CARACALLA BATHS

The **Caracalla Thermal Baths** are still easily recognizable, though they have been stripped of the marbles and works of art which made these one of the most sumptuous monuments of antiquity. The skeleton of the large complex of buildings reveals perfect architectural proportions and effective engineering solutions even in the external enclosure walls, designed on an almost perfect square plan (337m x 328m) which extends over a surface of as much as 120,000 sq.m.

*Bust of Emperor Caracalla. Aerial view of the Caracalla Baths as they are today and as they were originally.*

***The outdoor pool (natatio) of the Caracalla Baths.*** ➤

## > *A building revolution between Nero and the Flavii*

>>>>>>>>>>>>>>>>>>>>>>>>>>>>>>>>>>>>>>>>>>>>>>>>>>>>>>>>>>>>>>>>>>>

*Despite the efforts of the Flavii Emperors to erase all memory of Nero, not all his works were destroyed. From the piazza one could see, at the top of the Caelium Hill, the arcades of the aqueduct with which the despised Emperor had channelled water to the artificial lake of the Domus Aurea, now destroyed to make room for the amphitheatre. As always, Nero had paid particular attention to the aesthetics, realizing a series of arcades as slender as they were fragile, and which soon had to be reinforced. Quite different were the powerful series of traditional aqueducts standing for millenniums around Rome and many parts of Europe (see box below).*

*All memory of this, though, faded with the architectural revolution established in just a few years by Vespasian and continued by Titus in this vast area, object of admiration by the crowds, who proudly commented on the great building tradition of Rome (see box p. 46).*

page 48 >>

# ROME'S AQUEDUCTS

No other city of the ancient world was a thirsty as Rome where enormous efforts and money were spent to guarantee an adequate supply of water. A greatly emphasized testimony of this is the majestic rows of arcades along the consular roads of the south-east quadrant of the city, where the majority of the aqueducts came from.

The Romans recurred to this construction technique for a simple reason: the instruments available in those days made it definitely easier to channel water along the top of the arcades rather than dig kilometres of ditches in which to place the piping (like we do today). Furthermore, maintenance was in this way simpler and the water which flowed above ground in covered passages, was protected from all kinds of pollution.

The construction of these imposing works of engineering extended for centuries in the life of Rome, from 314 BC, when the Appian aqueduct, the oldest, was built, up to 226 AD when Emperor Septimius Severus had the eleventh, and last, Roman aqueduct built, known as the Alessandrino.

*Section of the Claudian aqueduct in the aqueduct park in Rome.*

**Aqueduct under construction. ➤**

# ANCIENT ROMANS, GIFTED BUILDERS

Since their very origins, the Romans dedicated particular attention to the solidity of their constructions, skilfully using various techniques in combining the materials (stones, bricks) beginning from the archaic *opus quadratum* (overlapping big blocks of squared stone), used since the 6th Century BC. When, between the 3rd and 2nd century BC the *opus coementicum* was introduced, apparently for reducing costs, the novelty was practically transformed into an innovative revolution which enabled Romans to construct buildings which where up to then unthinkable. The new technique used a mixture of gravel, stone chips and terracotta, held together with a liquid mortar which, when hardened gained highly resistant and at the same time flexible properties, unknown features in traditional materials.

One of the most brilliant architectural solutions feasible in cement building of the time was the frequent use of the vault and in general of the round section roof, the greatest example of which was the perfect dome of the **Pantheon** (see box p. 49). The

*Section of the Pantheon.*

cement technique was precious also in underwater construction, in building bridges and ports, as we are told by the greatest theoretician of Roman architecture, Vitruvius.

Also in building the Colosseum, the cement technique was of great help in the subterranean part, which still today presents a circular channel.

# THE PANTHEON

Built in around 28 BC by Marco Vipsanius Agrippa, a valiant Roman commander, friend and son in law of Emperor Augustus, the **Pantheon** was originally a temple dedicated to all the divinities of the Greco-Roman religion jointly with the dynastic cult of the *gens Julia*. One hundred and fifty years after it was built, it was completely rebuilt by Hadrian and it is in this version that we see it today. The traditional Augustan rectangular based edifice became a grand, round based hall surmounted by an unprecedented and audacious vault, preceded by a rectangular portico on the pediment of which Hadrian left the original inscription of the first builder. Inside the temple one can admire the rhythmic succession of vaults and arches that animate the circular base. At the centre of the dome is a large oculus 8.90m in diameter, only source of light, beautifully drawing the curved outline, thanks to a play of light and shadow of the niches on the walls. In the 7th Century the temple was turned into a Christian church and was preserved from destruction, surviving over centuries, unharmed.

*Example of opus coementicum. Aerial view of the Pantheon.*

## > **Entrance to the Colosseum**
>>>>>>>>>>>>>>>>>>>>>>>>>>>>>>

*The signals that the opening of the amphitheatre was imminent increased until an announcement by the banditores informed the crowd that the long wait was almost over: all were invited to have ready their previously distributed entrance tickets with the numbers that identified the entrance arches on the ground floor, which the spectators would approach.*

*The four arches corresponding to the main axes of the ellipse, reserved for the authorities, had no numbers, since the illustrious spectators were obsequiously accompanied to their seats; on the northern side, there was the entrance of honour, protected by a porch decorated with stuccos and frescos that led directly to the imperial tribune.*

*At this point the eager spectators would spend the last minutes before the games admiring the splendid architecture of the **Flavian Amphitheatre** (see box on p.49).*

(see box on p.49)

>>

*Arch no. 52, entrance to the Colosseum.*

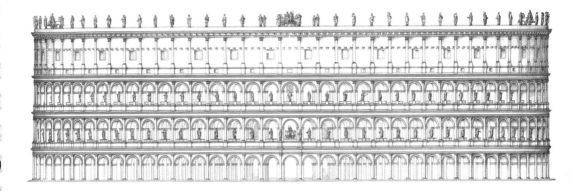

# THE ARCHITECTURE OF THE FLAVIAN AMPHITHEATRE

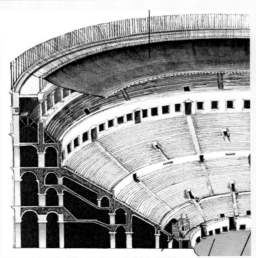

The majestic exterior of the **Colosseum**, faced in travertine stone, presented the most significant motif in Roman architecture in all its austere beauty: the joining of the arch to the architrave was enhanced in a compact rhythmical concept, varied by the succession of the three classical orders in the lateral semi-columns.

The solid Doric style was on the ground tier, the elegant Ionic on the first tier, the fanciful Corinthian on the second tier, the attic presented numerous consoles paired with holes for the crossed poles of the ingenious system that supported the amphitheatre's protective, enormous awning.

The complex mechanism was operated by a team of sailors from the port of Capo Miseno, in Campania. The arches were decorated with statues which have been almost completely lost.

*Architectural plan of the Colosseum (Busiri-Vici). Section of the Colosseum showing the structure of the awning.*

## > *The surprising interiors of the Colosseum*
>>>>>>>>>>>>>>>>>>>>>>>>>>>>>>>>>>>>>>>>>>>>>>>>>>>>>>>>>>>>>>

*Everyone, when entering, could see the vast arena that extended in the central part of the building, which on that day of the inauguration was not yet completed. It looked like a sort of basin which could have easily been filled with the water from the underground aquifer. For this first event though the basin would be covered by*

*wooden boarding on which the inaugural spectacle would take place.*

*In years to come, spectators could admire ship battles (naumachiae), like the ones that were held in other Roman venues.*

*It was only a few years after the inauguration of the Colosseum that Domitian built the complex underground network (see box on p. 51), which enabled a perfect organization of the entertainment.*

# ONE HUNDRED DAYS OF SPECTACLES

The hundred days for the celebrations of the inauguration of the Colosseum have been described to us by Roman authors of subsequent periods. About twenty years later Svetonius, in his "Life of Titus" writes that no less than five thousand wild animals were fought in just one day. About a century later instead, the historian Dion Cassius writes about a spectacular battle between cranes and four elephants and that about nine thousand animals and two thousand gladiators were killed. These weren't the only extraordinary numbers: under Trajan, in the *venationes* (hunts) held in the **Colosseum**, in 120 days, 11,000 animals from every part of the vast empire had fought for their lives

*Reconstruction of the Colosseum. Hunting scene (venatio) in the arena.*

# THE COLOSSEUM BASEMENTS

The amphitheatre's dense underground network of chambers and tunnels was used to host the games' protagonists, gladiators, beasts, and all that was necessary for the combats and hunts. This underground level extended throughout the whole area, divided into four quadrants by two large corridors that crossed in the centre. This enabled a perfect organization, thanks to which the games took place in the arena with maximum efficiency. There were even large hoists for lifting the beasts and the necessary equipment up to the arena level, while the gladiators used a passage that connected this underground area to the adjacent smaller amphitheatre, the *Ludus Magnus*, built for them to train in. Another underground level presented a ring shaped water piping connected to the aquifer which had generated Nero's lake; it was used, as well as for washing out the arena, also for the amazing water shows created before the construction of the underground level and described with admiration by the authors of the time, such as Svetonius, Martial, Dion Cassius.

*Reconstruction of the hoist mechanism in the Colosseum underground level.*

## > Opening day: animal hunts, executions and gladiator fights

>>>>>>>>>>>>>>>>>>>>>>>>>>>>>>>>>>>>>>>>>>>>>>>>>>>>>>>>>>>>>>>>>>>>>>

*Amongst the spectators, maybe the most attentive is the poet Martial who has the task of describing the exceptional program of spectacles performed on the inauguration of the imperial amphitheatre, which he calls the Colosseum, in one of his works, (the "De spectaculis") written to celebrate Titus. Animals were brought in from the most distant regions, mainly exotic animals, and were used for the hunts in the arena (venationes) that were always held on the first day. In the central hours of the day Martial describes in amazement an unprecedented use of wild animals, like killing "machines" for executing those who were sentenced to death, in spectacles inspired by*

*mythological tales. Years later, many of those sentenced to death were followers of Christianity (see box on p. 56), who were persecuted, though in actual fact these were less than what is generally believed.*

*The poet-chronicler is particularly impressed by the scene of the execution of a convict who, forced to play the part of Orpheus, the mythical musician who was able to placate wild beasts, and obviously not succeeding in the imitation was "torn to pieces by an ungrateful bear".*

*In the days that followed the central cavity would be filled with water and the spectators could admire mock sea battles (or* naumachiae*), popular since the times of Augustus (in the* naumachia *of Trastevere), as well as real aquatic shows.*

*Though the bloody games with the wild beast were very popular amongst the public, the favourite part of the show was the so called* munera, *the famous gladiator fights (see box on p. 57-58) which had important roots in the Roman tradition since the republican period.*

*This time the show was offered by the emperor and was therefore particularly grand: the celebrations for the opening of the Colosseum consisted in one hundred days of uninterrupted performances (see box on p.50).*

page 66 >>

*Painting by Jean-Léon Gérome, 1872, "Thumbs down".*

**The convict dressed as Orpheus in the arena, as described by the poet Martial.** ➤

# CHRISTIANITY AND THE ROMAN EMPIRE

Christianity spread to Rome very soon, under emperor Tiberius, who succeeded Augustus; but it was only with Nero's persecution that the first moments of crisis in the relations with the empire emerged. The return of political stability with Vespasian found the Roman Church in full organizational fervour; only in the last years of Domitian's reign did the persecution resume.

In the 2nd Century relations between the Church and the Empire went through alternate phases, and were sometimes even paradoxical. Under Trajan, who bore the honorary title of *optimus princeps*, they were accused and forced to hide, and even under the highly respected Marcus Aurelius, the philosopher emperor, the persecution was strongly resumed. On the contrary, under the detested Commodus, his successor, the Church incredibly experienced a period of peace. Only later, in the 3rd Century, when the soldier-emperors saw in Christianity a threat to the survival of the declining empire, the persecutions intensified. Not for long, though; only few years after the devastating persecutions under Domitian, in 313, with the edict of Milan, Constantine proclaimed the religious freedom of the Christians.

*Colossal marble head from the statue of Constantine, Palazzo dei Conservatori, Rome.*
*Painting of the Basilica of Constantine in the Vatican. Painting by H. Siemiradzki, 1899, "The future victims of the Colosseum".*

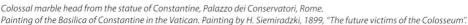

# THE GLADIATORS

There were two types of gladiators which can be defined in two fundamental categories: "heavy" and "light" combatants. The first were provided with the more traditional weaponry, consisting of, besides offensive weapons, also a considerable defence equipment (shield, helmet, protective padding for the limbs) whereas those of the second category privileged speed and were therefore equipped more essentially and sometimes in a bizarre manner. Of the first, the mirmillones, were armed with a short sword (the *gladius*) and protected by the *scutum*, a large rectangular shield similar to that of the legionaries. The weaponry of the traces (a curved blade sword, a shield and a crested helmet), was typical of their area of origin. The *secutores*, had to pursue particu-

*Combat between a Secutor and a Retiarius.*

larly the *retiarii*, though they had a weaponry similar to that of the *mirmillones*, their shield and armour was rounded which made it more difficult for the pursued retiarii to effectively use the nets they were supplied with along with trident and sword. A category all of itself was that of the *equites* who solemnly opened the games, entering the arena on horseback, clad in a tunic and armed with spear and

a long sword. Together with the *provocatores*, they had the "privilege" of fighting only against gladiators of their same class, whereas all other gladiator matches were fought between gladiators of different categories. At the opposite extreme we can place the tumultuous mass of the *catervarii*, who entered haphazardly into the arena transforming the typical duels into a disorderly brawl.

*Mosaic depicting combat scenes between gladiators supervised by referees. Combat between Murmillo and Traex. Bronze helmet worn by the mirmillones, from Pompeii, 1st Century AD, National Archaeological Museum of Naples.*

# GLADIATOR TRAINING AND LUDUS MAGNUS

While building the underground level of the Colosseum, indispensable for the realization of the most spectacular animal hunts and gladiator combats, Domitian built the largest gladiator school in Rome, the *Ludus Magnus*, adjacent to the amphitheatre. This was connected with the amphitheatre by an underground passage which led to the centre of the arena. There were about a thousand gladiators lodged in the *Ludus*, hosted in small cell-like rooms on three floors facing the courtyard which was designed like a miniature amphitheatre. Here the gladiators were trained for combat in the arena, through a tough physical and psychological preparation and a balanced, barley based diet, they had massage, regular medical checkups and, above all, a very intense training with blunt or wooden weapons (which weighed twice as much as the real thing), under the guidance of masters known as the *doctores*, usually former gladiators.

*The Ludus Magnus. Frieze decorated with gladiator scenes, Colosseum.*

**Double scene of the Colosseum arena with animal hunts (venatio) and ship battles (naumachia).** ➤

# > *The spectators take their seats in the amphitheatre*
>>>>>>>>>>>>>>>>>>>>>>>>>>>>>>>>>>>>>>>>>>>>>>>>>>>>>>>>>>>>>>

*The part of the cavea (see box on p. 67) for seating the public was characterized by an innovative system of steps, tunnels and passageways which were accessed in an orderly fashion from the entrance arches through ring shaped vaulted corridors that eased a smooth entrance and exit of the great mass of spectators.*
*The tickets indicated the seat numbers in the five sectors on the different tiers according to social rank and sex: the first was for senators and had marble steps; the others were in masonry, whereas the last was reserved for the lower class women and the steps were made of wood.*

>>

*Colosseum interior: general view and detail of the marble steps of the first sector.*

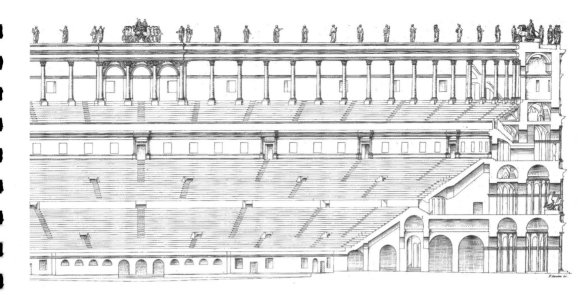

## THE CAVEA, A MIRROR OF SOCIETY

The seating arrangement reproduced the divisions of the Roman citizens in social classes, placed hierarchically in front of the emperor. From this layout the symbolic role of the Colosseum appears as a clear representation of Roman society. Violent contests were deeply rooted in the history of Rome: they celebrated the bloodshed over centuries in the conquest wars which had made Rome the capital of the world.

This had been the scope of the first gladiator games in the republican age, held in makeshift, wooden amphitheatres.

In the imperial age, combat was left to the gladiators who, though despised socially, had become true stars, the surviving symbols of charismatic virility. Author Seneca spoke of them as the only, new examples of strength and courage in the face of death.

*Cross section of the Colosseum (Busiri-Vici).*
*Model of a cross section of a segment of the Colosseum.*

## > *After the show, more praise to Titus*

>>>>>>>>>>>>>>>>>>>>>>>>>>>>>>>>>>>>>>>>>>>>>>>>>

*Amongst the seventy thousand spectators pouring out of the amphitheatre, comments on the incredible event alternated with words of praise for Titus, whose popularity was already solidly founded on his much admired actions of the previous year. Two dramatic events had given him the opportunity to express his love for his people: the frightful eruption of the Vesuvius, that had destroyed Pompeii and Herculaneum, and a violent fire that ravaged Rome, which many considered as serious as Nero's in 64 AD. Many stated with conviction that the generous sovereign had accelerated the opening of the Colosseum to compensate the citizens for these tragedies. Some instead recalled the grand military triumphs on the Sacred Way (see box on p. 70), celebrated by emperor Vespasian and by his son Titus after the conquest of Jerusalem. This historic feat by the Roman army (see box on p.74-76) would be immortalized in marble a few years later by Titus' brother and successor Domitian, in the reliefs on the arch raised at the end of the Sacred Way facing the amphitheatre.*

page 78 >>

*Coin with the image of Vespasian. Statue of Titus. Arch of Titus on the Sacred Way.*
*"Grande Ludovisi" marble sarcophagus, with scenes of battle between Romans and Barbarians, 3rd century AD, Palazzo Altemps, Rome.*

# MILITARY TRIUMPHS ON THE SACRED WAY

The **Sacred Way** was, from the beginning of the victorious Roman wars, the final leg of the processions celebrating the return of the military from the campaigns fought all around the known world.

With their taste for spectacular events, the Romans flocked in masses along the most important road of the city, the Sacred Way, where the glorious parade took place following precise rules.

Fundamental was the presence of the subjugated enemies, especially if these were people of fame.

The long procession was headed by the military chief, who in imperial times was the Emperor himself, preceded by the spoils of war. Then came the parade of the prisoners of war, who in Titus' triumph in the Judaic war were made to re-enact, like in a theatrical performance, some phases of the lost battles. But ancient Roman wisdom provided also that there be a servant standing at the side of the conqueror who, as he held a crown over his master's head would repeat in his ear: "Remember that you are just a man" or "Look behind you". The ceremony ended in the temple of Capitoline Jupiter, where the victor returned the robes and symbols of sovereignty that pertained to the divine statue, which he was allowed to wear on celebrating his victorious role.

*The sacred Way with the Arch of Titus on the background. Bas relief of the triumph of Marcus Aurelius, Palazzo dei Conservatori, Rome.*
**The procession of Emperor Marcus Aurelius on the Sacred Way in 176 AD, to celebrate the triumph over the Germanic populations. ➤**

Rome was able to found the largest and most long-lived empire in history also thanks to its ability to transform over time its formidable army.

In the royal period, the army's structure was based on the legion (300 soldiers) which was divided into centuries (groups of 100 conscripts with personal armament).

The Roman army inherited the phalanx formation from the Greeks and the Etruscans, which consisted in a compact front of heavily armed infantry in the middle flanked by the cavalry. At the beginning of the republican period the legion was divided into maniples, agile and autonomous tactical units. In the Punic Wars the naval fleet (*classis*) was introduced.

With the expansion of the empire also the number of legions began to grow, increasing from 2 to 60 at the end of the civil wars. In this expansionist phase one of the reasons for the primacy of the Roman army was the fact that each citizen (from 18 to 46 years of age) was also a soldier, continuously undergoing tough training and provided with a strong sense of ownership of the city which, with his own contribution, would dominate the world.

In 107 BC, Gaius Marius' military reform introduced the cohort (deriving from the union of three maniples) and voluntary military service; this introduced the figure of the salaried soldier which the state provided with a uniform armament consisting of the *gladius* (the short sword), *pilum* (spear), shield, helmet, cuirass and greaves.

During the imperial period, the army changed its organization adapting it to the different situations, varying the number of legions (on average between 25 and 35). These, formed by 6,000 units each, were divided into 10 cohorts which were subdivided into centuries (80 soldiers), each formed by 10 *contubernia* (groups of 8 men).

2

*Scene of the Roman siege of a Gallic fortress, using crossbows (1) catapults (2), testudo formations (3), rams (4), siege tower (5).*

Contributing to this perfect organization was the presence of experts and technicians, thanks to whom the great military conquests were always combined with works of advanced civil engineering such as aqueducts, bridges and roads (see box on p. 77), strengthening Roman presence in the territories in times of peace and spreading cultural Romanization.

This great technical mastery also made the many war machines remarkably efficient , be these siege instruments (such as the ram and the tower) or artillery (such as the ballista and the catapult).

# MILITARY HIERARCHY

The principal figures in military hierarchy were the *legatus* (legion commander), the *tribunus* (one of the six officers under the *legatus*), the centurion (who lead the century), the legionary (infantry soldier), the mounted soldier and the auxiliary soldier (who did not have Roman citizenship).

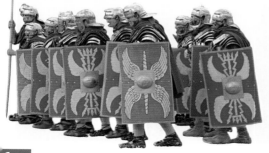

*Legionaries advancing in formation.*

*Statue of a Roman legionary.*

# CIVIL ENGINEERING: BUILDING OF ROADS

The deepest layer (*statumen*) consisted of a cobblestone base, on top of that was a layer of sand (*rudus*), sometimes mixed with clay. The third layer (*nucleus*) was a lining made of crushed stone and gravel. The road was then finished with a final surface layer (*summum dorsum*), made of slabs of faced stone fitted into place. The paved roads were thus resistant to the continuous passage of carts, water, ice and wear and tear of time.

# > One step forward in history: the grand Rome of the Flavii

>>>>>>>>>>>>>>>>>>>>>>>>>>>>>>>>>>>>>>>>>>>>>>>>>>>>>>>>

*The crowds pouring out of the amphitheatre could not yet admire the arch on the Sacred Way, which ten years later would be dedicated to Titus by his brother Domitian. Titus' successor will continue, like his predecessors to link his more significant urban works to the Romans' passion for sports.*

*Even the royal **palace of the Flavii** on the Palatine hill (see box on p. 79) overlooks the **Circus Maximus**, the oldest and grandest sports arena in ancient Rome. Years later **Domitian's Stadium** would be built in Campus Martius; its oblong shape is still visible in the 21st Century in the unmistakable planimetry of Piazza Navona that has replaced it.*  >>

*The Domitian Stadium and the present day Piazza Navona.*

# THE FLAVIAN PALACE ON THE PALATINE

Since its construction, the splendid residence of the Flavii, described by the poet Martial as "one of the most beautiful things in the world", was the object of much admiration. It rose on a spacious flat area created to fill the gully between two hills, the imperial hill (the Germalus) and the actual **Palatine**.

There was a succession of halls, exedras, porches with fountains and pools, huge panoramic terraces, powerful substructures. In the official part of the palace (the *Domus Flavia*) one can admire the *triclinium*, the dining room known as the *Cenatio Iovis*, followed by a characteristic octagonal labyrinth with mirror-like walls, which probably served to watch one's back against eventual assaults during the emperor's afternoon stroll. Amongst the

other official halls was the *aula regia* (the so called Basilica), where the emperor held his proceedings and where the imperial council would meet. The ruins of the palace's private apartments (the *Domus Augustana*), extend to the external area of the compound, this was a building on various floors with terraces from which the imperial court could watch the spectacles held in the Circus Maximus.

The regal complex is completed to the east by emperor Domitian's Palatine circus, an oblong arena surrounded by a multi-storey colonnade (with the large imperial podium or *pulvinar* overlooking the arena), an example in reduced size of that which will be the same emperor's great stadium (see box on p. 78).

*Above, the Circus of Emperor Domitian on the Palatine. Below, the octagonal labyrinth at the back of the triclinium of the Domus Flavia.*

## > *The Romans' passion for sports: chariot races*

*The crowds flowed towards the south–eastern part of the city, along the Triumphalis road until they reached the Circus Maximus, the ancient sports grounds that held the Romans' favourite sports event, the chariot race (see box below). Unfortunately, for the past fifteen years the circus has been closed due to the lengthy works needed to repair the serious damage caused by Nero's fire, in 64 AD which had almost completely destroyed entire districts. Also for this reason, the news of the opening of the amphitheatre had attracted large crowds of fans, eager to show their sports enthusiasm in the new games.*

>>

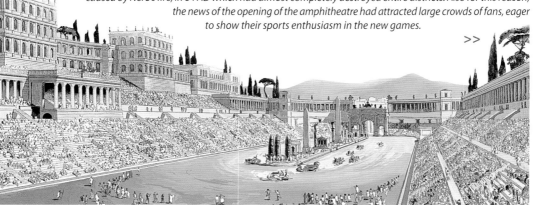

## CHAMPIONS AND SUPPORTERS

For many years the chariot races with the bigae (drawn by two horses, for beginners) and the quadrigas (drawn by four horses, for the more expert contestants) attracted hoards of supporters from Rome and from the cities of the empire, with events held in the numerous festivities of the year (at least one hundred and eighty in the imperial period). The cheering was similar to that of today and the charioteers, hailed by the crowds, were true stars, who would not hesitate to recur to foul play in order to obtain victory, even at the cost of the opponents' lives. The teams were traditionally four – like the seasons – and were distinguished by the colours white, green, red and blue.

In Rome, the greatest support was given to the greens: to favour these emperor Caligula did not hesitate to poison the adversary charioteers. Again in the 4th Century, author Ammianus Marcellinus describes Roman supporters: "For the Romans, the Circus Maximus is temple and home in one. Many spend sleepless nights, anxious for the results of the races..."

*Event at the Circus Maximus. Massive marble statue of a chariot, 1st Century AD, Vatican Museums.*
**Chariot race in Circus Maximus.** ➤

## > **Other shows**
>>>>>>>>>>>>>>>>>>>>>>>>>

*A short distance away from Circus Maximus, another building witnessed moments of collective passion: the theatre performances (see box below).*

*The **Theatre of Marcellus** could seat up to 20,000 people and its splendid architecture inspired the architects of the Colosseum. For many decades (it was opened in 12 AD) it was one of the most popular venues for the Romans who still fondly remembered its namesake Marcus Claudius Marcellus, Augustus' nephew and designated heir, who died in his early twenties, celebrated and mourned by Rome's greatest poet, Virgil.*

>>

# ROMAN THEATRE

Whereas in the Greek world the theatre was one of the city's most important public events, with profound religious implications, the theatre in Rome struggled to achieve a significant place in the rigid republican society. In theatrical performances (which began in 364 BC) theatre was mixed with other forms of entertainment, such as gladiator fights. The theatre in Rome was therefore more confined to the entertainment ambit, apart from a literary endeavour in imitating the great Greek tragedies and plays. But the most popular was the folk theatre of Italic origin like the farce and the *atellana* (from *Atella*, a town in the Campania region), with fixed characters similar to the later stock characters of the *Commedia dell'Arte*.

The construction of grand theatres favoured, also in the imperial period, the realization of performances in which the scenery was more important than the literary text. The kind of performances which were most popular with the Romans continued to be mime theatre and pantomime, often spiced up by female strippers.

*Mosaic of musicians on stage, from Cicero's Villa in Pompeii, 1ˢᵗ Century AD. The Theatre of Marcellus. Stone theatre mask.*
**Representation of a performance at the Ancient Ostia theatre. ➤**

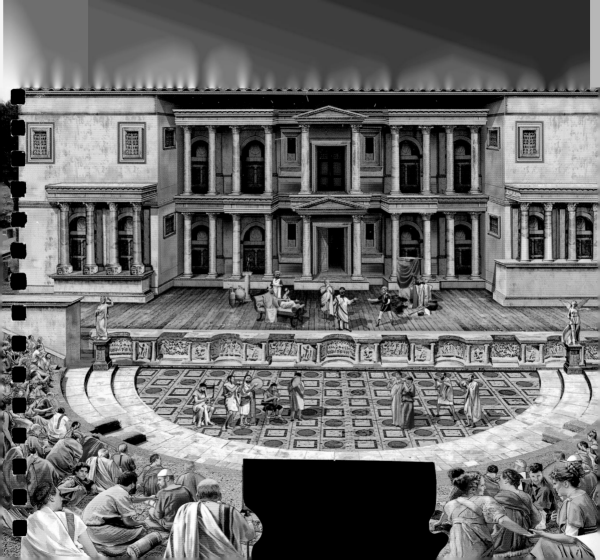

# > *Going home*

>>>>>>>>>>>>>>>>>>>>>>>>>>>>>>>>>>>>>>>>>>>>>>>>>>>>>>>>>>>>>>>>>>>>>>>>>>>>>>

*After commenting on the show, the spectators headed towards their homes, which were quite different from one another. The passion for sports that had made them as one and the same in the large* cavea *gave way to the social differences; the privileged of the first marble steps returned to the splendid isolation of their* domus *(see box p. 90-91), whereas the majority of spectators returned to the* insulae *(see box on p. 92), their crammed plebeian housing. In many areas of Rome one would find both types of homes. In particular, on nearby Aventine Hill, the* insulae *were gradually replaced by splendid, elegant* domus, *mixed amongst temples dedicated to Roman divinities and foreign cults. And not by chance: since the times of the kings, this secluded hill had been populated by the citizens of territories conquered by Rome. Looming over the hill's aura in the first stages of the city's life, was the fact that it was on this Aventine hill that Remus, according to tradition, lost his divine battle which allowed Romulus, from the Palatine hill opposite to be the only founder of Rome and it's first king.*

>>

*Entrance in the atrium of a domus.*

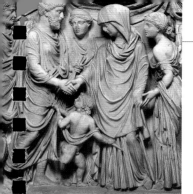

# THE FAMILY IN ANCIENT ROME

In the approximate thousand years of Roman history, the family nucleus changed according to the changes in society. What didn't change was the fundamental figure of the *pater familias*, who in ancient times had absolute authority, to the point of having the right to dispose of the lives of his children. And daughters remained subjugated for life, passing from the father's authority, who gave them in marriage at a very young age, from 12, to that of the husband, the new *pater familias*. During the republican period, though they had no rights, women assumed importance in virtue of their maternal role.

Under Augustus it was finally decided to give marriage a complete juridical form with consequent reduction of the archaic absolute power of the *pater familias*. Since then the Roman family took on a different character, closer to what it is today. The archaic structure of the aristocratic families, based on a large family nucleus comprising sons and daughters and their families and by the slaves was thus surpassed.

# ROMAN NAMES

For the Romans, the name indicated the bearer's social status. For free male citizens the formula was onomastic, known as *tria nomina*, and consisted in three elements: the *prenomen*, which was given to the newborn at birth; the *nomen gentilicum*, or the family name, which corresponds to today's surname; the *cognomen*, definitely adopted only in the 1st Century BC, which would be associated to a personal characteristic, birthplace or various activities.

The free woman instead received the gentilitial name, and later, from the latter republican period onwards, the father's *cognomen* in the female gender, often in the diminutive form.

Slaves had a single name, similar to a nickname which derived from a distinctive characteristic of the bearer.

The freed slaves instead, or freedmen, often took on their former master's *nomen* adding it to their original name.

*Detail of the sarcophagus with wedding scene, Museo Ducale, Mantova.*
*Funeral inscription for Lucius Julius Eudoxus, in the church of San Silvestro in Capite, Rome.*

# ARISTOCRATIC HOMES: THE DOMUS

The homes of the wealthy Romans, the *domus*, have obviously changed over the course of time, but there were certain recurring elements which we refer to here.

There were no openings onto the outside apart from the entrance which led to the *vestibulum*, an anti-chamber which was usually crowded with *clientes*. Then there was the *atrium*, an open space which received light and water from an aperture called the *compluvium*; water was collected in a basin below known as the *impluvium*. An important element of the *atrium* was the *lararium*, a domestic shrine with images of ancestors (*lares*). To the sides of the *atrium* were the *cubicula*, minute rooms used mainly as bedrooms; to the end, in front of the entrance, was the *tablinum*, a large office of the master of the house, which completed the "public" part of the *domus*.

Behind was the *peristilium*, the heart of the house, a porch enriched with plants, statues, vases and mosaics. The best rooms looked onto this porch, starting from the *triclinium*, the dining room that derives its name from the *triclinia*, beds on which the wealthy Romans lay when banqueting.

*Interior structure of a domus. Above, the triclinium in a domus.*

On the lateral wings of the peristyle were the smaller rooms, amongst which the *cubicula* of medium size, whereas at the end, facing the *tablinum*, was the exedra, a large hall for receptions and banquets for a large number of guests.
The kitchen instead was placed where space was found for it, usually adjacent to the latrine, since both used the same plumbing system.

*Frescoes in the triclinium of the so called Villa Livia on the Palatine, Rome.*
*Statue of Livia (wife of emperor Augustus).*

# HOMES OF THE COMMON PEOPLE: THE INSULAE

From the 4th Century BC, a different kind of housing was built for the common people, unlike the *domus* these were much taller but modest and above all cheap.

They were known as the *insulae*, buildings on various floors which could house a large number of families.

Due to the growing need for building sites because of the constant increase in the urban population, tall buildings were built on more floors but they were built with cheap materials so they were not too safe.

For this reason Augustus ordered that the *insulae* be limited to a maximum height of about twenty one metres (about seven floors of today), which Trajan then reduced to eighteen metres. The insula had many windows, some even with balconies. The ground floor had a portico with shops.

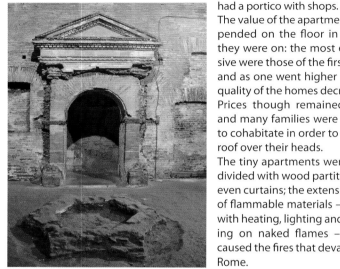

The value of the apartments depended on the floor in which they were on: the most expensive were those of the first floor, and as one went higher up the quality of the homes decreased. Prices though remained high and many families were forced to cohabitate in order to have a roof over their heads.

The tiny apartments were subdivided with wood partitions or even curtains; the extensive use of flammable materials – along with heating, lighting and cooking on naked flames – often caused the fires that devastated Rome.

# FIRE FIGHTERS IN ANCIENT ROME

Due to the frequent fires in Rome, emperor Augustus organized a network of fire fighters who, divided in seven cohorts of seven thousand men, had the task of fighting fires and guaranteeing citizens' safety.

Amongst the vigils were the *acquari*, who were in charge of the water pumps, the *balnearii*, specialized in interventions in the thermal baths and, those whom we would today define as police forces, the *carcerarii* and the *quaestionarii*, the latter being in charge of interrogations. There were also the *sebaciarii*, whose existence is attested by ancient graffiti found on the walls of the only remaining barracks, the ones in Trastevere, which appear to have been in charge of night services to the light of the *sebum* (tallow) torches.

*Barracks (excubitorium) of the vigiles of the seventh cohort in the district of Trastevere, Rome.*

**Fire in the district of the insula of the Aurighi, Ancient Ostia. ➤**

# CONSULAR ROADS AND OTHER ROMAN ROADS

Romans took particular care of their roads, first amongst all the consular roads, which from the time of the construction of the Appian Way, in 312 BC, fanned out from Rome to all the territories of the constantly growing empire. These were usually paved roads (*viae silice stratae*), safe and resistant, whereas a second category of roads consisted in roads that had a simple layer of gravel (*viae glarea stratae*). Finally, there were also dirt roads (*viae terrenae*), in which one would be inevitably bogged down in the rainy season and covered in dust in the hot dry season. All the *viae*, whatever their surface, enabled the contemporary transit of two carts heading in opposite directions.

There were minor roads, like the *actus*, a narrower road, banned to carts but open to pedestrians, litters and horses, or the *iter*, which would be transited on foot or in a litter, without the use of animals.

*Suburban stretch of the Old Appian Way (Via Appia Antica).*

# SEPULCHRES ALONG THE APPIAN WAY

In observance of the ancient laws of Rome concerning burial grounds which ruled that tombs had to be built outside the city walls, the extra-city roads were flanked with sepulchres, destined to host the deceased members of wealthy families. Quite different was the fate of the slaves and the more humble classes, who were thrown into mass graves, dug principally in the Esquiline hill. Amongst the consular roads the *Appian Way* is the one that has the best preserved series of monumental sepulchres flanking it, also due to the fact that, after traffic routes were detoured and the area had been left to grow wild in the 16th Century, after the construction of the *Via Appia Nuova*, it was restored in the first half of the 19th Century.

## ROMAN FUNERAL RITUALS

As elsewhere, funerals in Rome were strictly dependent on the social class of the deceased. Ceremonies of important families were arranged by the *libitinarii*, who organized the sumptuous celebrations paid for by the family. The deceased was exposed for a few days in the entrance hall of the home, with a coin under the tongue to pay Charontes the ferryman for the passage to the afterlife. From here the funeral procession set off, opened by mimes, dancers and musicians; there were also the "moaners", women hired to accompany the ceremony with their laments. The procession reached the sepulchre which was outside the city walls. The more modest classes were organized in associations, the *collegia funeraticia*, which were created for the purpose of guaranteeing a decent burial, thanks to a common fund allocated with the contributions of the members. Whatever the rank of the deceased, cremation was the preferred choice. The ashes were collected in an urn, placed in a collective sepulchre known as the *columbarium*. Interment remained the only option for the poor and the slaves, until it became prevalent with the spreading of Christianity.

*Sepulchre in the archaeological park of the tombs of Via Latina, Rome. Roman urn of the 1st Century AD of Lucius Cornelius Letus.*
**Reconstruction of Imperial Rome (4th Century AD), Museum of Roman Civilization, Rome.** ➤

# THE MONARCHY

According to the calculations of historian M. Terentius Varro (116-27 BC), Rome was founded on April 21, 753 BC.

After its foundation, Rome was governed by kings (753-510 BC); it was then a Republic, lead by consuls (510-30 BC), and finally an empire (27 BC- 476 AD).

*During the monarchic period, Rome conquers its domination over the Latin peoples dispossessing the ancient sacred city Albalonga.*

**First period (753 – 617 BC):**
According to tradition, the first four kings to reign, alternately Roman and Sabine, were: Romulus, Numa Pompilius, Tulius Hostilius, Ancus Marcius.

**Second period (616 – 510 BC):**
The last three kings, Tarquinius Priscus, Servius Tulius, Tarquinius Superbus, mark the Etruscan period of the Roman monarchy.

**509 BC** With the deposition of King Tarquinius, accused of the death of virtuous patrician Lucretia, the long period of Etruscan influence on Rome ends.

# THE REPUBLIC

*The Republic continues its growing expansion of Rome, first in the Italian peninsula and then all over Europe and the Mediterranean coasts (the Mare nostrum of the Romans).*

**First period (510-87 BC):**
dall'espulsione di Tarquinio alla dittatura di Silla.

**494 BC** Beginning of the conflicts between patricians and plebeians.
**451 BC** Publication of the first written laws (the XII tablets).
**396 BC** Rome destroys Veio, subduing southern Etruria.
**390 BC** The Gauls, under Brennus, after invading and devastating Rome are forced to retreat to their territories. Rome, after a slow but constant reconstruction, resumes its expansion.
**343-290 BC** With the Samnite wars, Rome begins to extend its influence on the Campania region and on the entire south of Italy.
**326 BC** The conquest of Naples marks Rome's expansion in Magna Grecia.
**264-146 BC** With the three Punic wars Rome wins the battle for supremacy of the Mediterranean with Carthage being forced to accept the harshest peace conditions which cancel it from the maps of history.
**222 BC** Rome occupies Cisalpine Gaul (northern Italy).
**146 BC** Conquest of Greece.
**133-121 BC** The Gracchi brothers pay with their lives for attempting more political and social rights to the plebeians.
**107 BC** A military reform is promoted by Caius Marius, who obtains brilliant victories in Africa against the Germanic populations of the Cimbri and the Teutons. Leading the democratic party, he takes over power in Rome.

**91-89 BC** The Italics revolt to obtain Roman citizenship (social war).
**88 BC** Sulla, leader of the aristocratic party, attacks Marius thus starting the civil war, which has Rome devastated by a succession of victories, defeats and bloody vendettas. With the death of Marius (85 BC), Sulla becomes unrivalled.

**Second period (87-30 BC):** the Republic's crisis from Sulla to Augustus.

**82-79 BC** With Sulla's dictatorship the crisis of the republican institutions is accentuated; laws enforced by the democratic party in favour of plebeians are abolished.
**67 BC** Pompey, the new aristocratic leader, obtains important military victories.
**69-59 BC** Julius Caesar rises in his political career, from Quaestor to Pontifex Maximus to Consul, as leader of the democratic party.
**60-53 BC** Caesar seals a private political agreement with Pompey and the wealthy Crassus, profoundly changing the political situation. Thus the first triumvirate is established.
**58 - 51 BC** Caesar conducts a victorious military campaign in Gaul; between 55 and 54 BC, he leads an expedition to Britain.
**51 BC** Caesar falls out with Pompey. Caesar returns to Rome against the dispositions of the Senate which sides with Pompey.
**49 BC** After the failure of the triumvirate and the killing of Pompey in Pharsalus, Caesar seizes control as a dictator.
**44 BC** After extending his dictatorship to a lifelong position, on March 15 (the Ides of March), Julius Caesar is killed by the republican conspirators in the Senate hall.
**43 BC** Octavian, Caesar's nephew and heir is elected Consul and forms a second triumvirate with Mark Anthony and Lepidus.
**42 BC** In the battle of Philippi, Octavian defeats the republican conspirators who had killed Julius Caesar.
**31 BC** Failure of the second triumvirate; in the conflict that follows, Octavian defeats Mark Anthony at Actium (Greece).
**27 BC** The Roman Senate confers Octavian the highest republican offices and the title of Augustus. The republic ends here.

6

**27 BC** Augustus brings radical changes to the organization of the empire, leaving apparently intact, however, the many republican institutions. Despite some military defeats in Germany, the Augustan period coincides with the golden century of Roman culture: contemporaries of this period are authors such as Cicero, Virgil, Lucretius, Horatio, Ovid, Livy, Tacitus. The birth of Jesus Christ under the princedom of Augustus marks the beginning of the Christian age.

**14 AD** At the death of Augustus, the rise to the throne of his adopted son Tiberius marks the beginning of the dynastic succession of the Julio-Claudian family. Imperial prestige is strengthened with the start of the process of the divinization of the emperor.

**41 AD** Emperor Caligula is killed at only 29, for having attempted to introduce the absolute power of the oriental sovereigns to Rome, removing the senate.

**64 AD** Under Nero (54-68) the city is devastated by a huge fire which the Christians are blamed for. During the persecution that follows, Saint Peter and Saint Paul are martyred.

**68 AD** The Julio-Claudian dynasty ends with Nero's violent death.

**72 AD** The Flavian dynasty begins with Vespasian who, together with his son Titus, wins the Judaic war and conquers Jerusalem. The new emperors bestow the city with grand public buildings, such as the Colosseum.

**80 AD** The huge amphitheatre is inaugurated by Titus, son and successor of Vespasian.

**96 AD** Domitian, though he had built the grand palace on the Palatine and a number of impressive works, did not enjoy the favour of his people as his father and brother had. The Flavian dynasty ends with his violent death.

**98-117 AD.** Under Trajan the Roman Empire reaches its maximum expansion.

**117-138 AD** Hadrian consolidates the boundaries of the empire. He encourages the spreading of Hellenic culture, raising Rome to the heights of its splendour.

**193 AD** The new Severan dynasty, which began with the African Septimius Severus, marks the new role of the provinces.

**212 AD** Caracalla, son of Septimius Severus, extends Roman citizenship to all the subjects of the empire.

**233 AD** With the killing of the last of the Severus dynasty, a profound crisis befalls the empire, which leads to the military emperors taking power.

**250 AD** Emperor Decius starts the great persecutions of the Christians, accused of being the cause of the empire's crisis because they refused to worship Roman divinities.

**272 AD** Construction of the Aurelian Walls to defend Rome from the Barbaric invasions.

**285 AD** Diocletian tries to end the empire's crisis by dividing it into four regions (tetrarchia).
The complex succession mechanism which he created, however, causes irremediable conflicts between the pretenders.

**313 AD** With Constantine, victorious over his rival Massentium in Ponte Milvio (312), in the last of the conflicts that followed the tetrarchy of Diocletian, Christianity wins the challenge of the persecutions thanks to the proclamation of freedom of religion decreed with the Milan Edict.

**331 AD** Constantine transfers his court to Bisantium (Constantinople) and Rome is no longer capital of the empire.

**395 AD** The Roman Empire is divided into East (under emperor Arcadius) and West (under emperor Honorius).

**410 and 455 AD** Rome is sacked by the Goths under Alaric and by Vandals under Genseric.

**476 AD** Odoacre, commander of the Barbaric troops associated to the Roman army, puts an end to the Western Roman Empire, deposing the young emperor Romulus Augustulus and sending the imperial insignia to Constantinople.

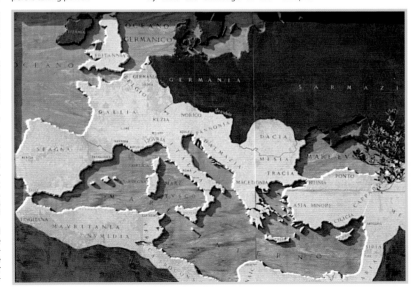

# INDEX

© **2012 ARCHEOLIBRI s.r.l.**
Via della Magliana 74/E - Roma (Italy)
Tel. +39 06 96.84.43.87 - Fax. +39 06 96.84.43.88
**www.archeolibri.com - info@archeolibri.com**
*Gruppo Lozzi Editori • www.gruppolozzi.it*

**"Everyday life in Imperial Rome"**
ISBN 9788866680796
**PATENTED SYSTEM**

Texts by: Maria Antonietta Lozzi Bonaventura. Editing and iconographic research: Fabiana Benetti.
Graphic reconstructions created for Archeolibri by Ricerca Due, Florence.
Photos: Archeolibri srl, Editrice Millenium srl, Lozzi Roma sas.
Translations: TperTradurre srl, Rome
Attached DVD "Ancient Rome, a Virtual Tour from Colosseum to St. Peter", produced by MyMax for Archeolibri.
Original music composed by Fernando Stefanucci for Archeolibri.

Printed by: C.S.C. Grafica s.r.l. - Guidonia (RM)

*The publisher is at the disposal of all right holders with whom it has not been possible to communicate, for any eventual involuntary omissions or inaccuracies in quoting the sources and/or photos..*

**PRODOTTO IN ITALIA**
**MADE IN ITALY**